Contents

Seaside sounds

At the seaside, there are lots of things to see, hear...

Seaside
Senses

Paul Humphrey

Photography by Chris Fairclough

W
FRANKLIN WATTS
LONDON•SYDNEY

First published in 2006 by
Franklin Watts
338 Euston Road
London NW1 3BH

Franklin Watts Australia
Hachette Children's Books
Level 17/207 Kent Street
Sydney NSW 2000

© 2006 Franklin Watts

ISBN: 0 7496 6610 2 (hbk)
ISBN: 0 7496 6854 7 (pbk)

Dewey classification number: 612.8

A CIP catalogue record for this book is available
from the British Library.

Planning and production by Discovery Books Limited
Editor: Rachel Tisdale
Designer: Ian Winton
Photography: Chris Fairclough
Series advisors: Diana Bentley MA and Dee Reid MA,
Fellows of Oxford Brookes University

The author, packager and publisher would like to thank the following
people for their participation in this book: Auriel Austin-Baker; Arrandeep Bola
and family; Lucas Tisdale.

Printed in China

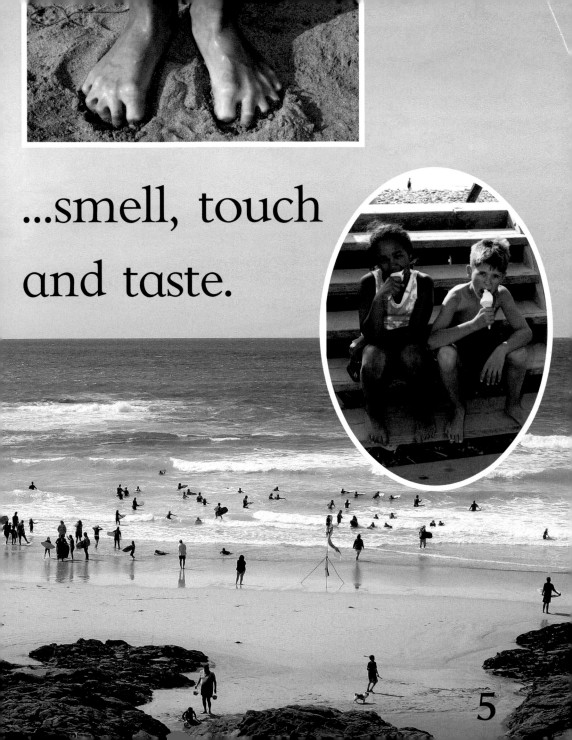

...smell, touch and taste.

5

You can see beach huts painted in bright colours...

...and a kite flying in the breeze.

shells and pebbles

Look at the colours
of the shells
and pebbles.

9

Crashing waves

You can hear waves rolling onto the shore...

...or crashing on
the rocks.

11

Seaside sounds

You can hear a seagull calling...

...and people laughing
and shouting.

Seaside smells

You can smell seaweed...

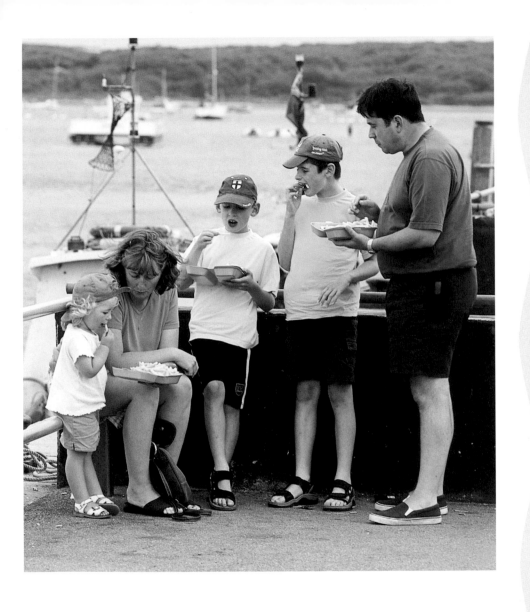

...and fish and chips!

Rough and smooth

The rocks feel rough.

But the pebbles
are smooth.

Cold and hot

The sea feels so cold...

...but the sun is hot.

Wind and sand

You can feel the wind in your hair...

...and the sand
under your feet.

Salty and sweet

The sea is salty...

...but ice cream tastes lovely and sweet!

Word bank

Look back for these words and pictures.

Beach huts

Ice cream

Kite

Pebbles

Rocks

Seagull

Seaweed

Shells

Waves